Welcome to Christ

Sponsors Guide

Augsburg Fortress

Minneapolis

Welcome to Christ: Sponsors Guide
Copyright © 2002 Augsburg Fortress. All rights reserved. Except for brief quotations in critical articles or reviews, no part of this book may be reproduced in any manner without prior written permission from the publisher. Write to: Permissions, Augsburg Fortress, Box 1209, Minneapolis, MN 55440-1209.
Or visit www.augsburgfortress.org/copyrights

This resource includes material first published in *Lutheran Book of Worship*, copyright © 1978, and *With One Voice*, copyright © 1995 Augsburg Fortress.

Writer: Beverly Piro
Editors: Robert Buckley Farlee and Becky Lowe
Cover art: Tanja Butler

Also available:
Welcome to Christ: A Lutheran Introduction to the Catechumenate ISBN 0-8066-3393-X
Welcome to Christ: A Lutheran Catechetical Guide ISBN 0-8066-3394-8
Welcome to Christ: Lutheran Rites for the Catechumenate ISBN 0-8066-3395-6
Welcome to Christ: Preparing Adults for Baptism and Discipleship
    (video) ISBN 6-0000-9043-9
What Do You Seek? Welcoming the Adult Inquirer ISBN 0-8066-4031-6

The paper used in this publication meets the minimum requirements of American National Standards for Information Sciences—Permanence of Paper for Printed Library materials, ANSI Z329.48-1984.

Manufactured in the USA.   ISBN 0-8066-4032-4
09 08 07 06 05 04 03 02   1 2 3 4 5 6 7 8 9 10

Contents

Introduction	4
A thumbnail sketch of the catechumenate process	8
What is a sponsor?	12
What does a sponsor do?	14
How are sponsor matches made?	19
Congregational support for sponsors	21
Sponsorship and renewal	23
Affirmation of baptism	25
A final word	27
Top ten ideas for sponsors	28
Appendix A: Excerpt from *The Use of the Means of Grace*	29
Appendix B: Resources for prayer	30

Introduction

The hymn of the day is being sung and groups of people are moving toward the front of the sanctuary. They gather around the baptismal font. They are young and old. They are singles, couples, and families. They have come to this Christian community in search of faith and fullness of life. They are about to receive the sign of the cross on their bodies: forehead, eyes, ears, lips, heart, shoulders, hands, and feet. Each stands face to face with a member of the congregation, whose hands trace the cross and touch the shoulders in blessing. This journey into Christianity is communal by its very nature. From beginning to end, accompanied by sponsors, taught by catechists, shepherded by clergy, and prayed for by the congregation, candidates for baptism or affirmation of baptism are never "going it alone." They have come to prepare themselves to receive the sacrament of Holy Baptism or to affirm their baptism, and in the process they are embraced by the community of the faithful.

Dear Sponsor,

You have been asked to sponsor an adult who desires to explore the Christian faith. The invitation has been extended to you because, like the person you will sponsor, you are on a journey of faith. You may have been on this faith road for your whole life or you may have come to faith more recently. Either way, you are invited to walk along in the process as a sponsor and companion to another person.

What is a sponsor? Consider yourself to be like a carpenter and the inquirer like an apprentice. A journey-level carpenter has more experience with the trade than an apprentice, but still will encounter challenges and make mistakes. The more experienced carpenter, though, might recognize the mistake sooner than the apprentice and may have learned to avoid some pitfalls. Invite the apprentice in faith to learn from you and with you.

As a sponsor, you will help to welcome the inquirer into the community of faith. You are asked to give of yourself as you worship, study scripture, pray, and in other ways live your faith. Receive your candidate with an open heart and be willing to share your own heart. You might be surprised at some of the things you say as you share your faith story with your candidate. Undoubtedly your faith will grow.

You will enter this time of sponsorship supported and prayed for by your catechumenate team and the congregation. Your pastor and catechumenate leaders will be available to you as resources and support. God has chosen you for the work of making disciples and God will give you the strength, the wisdom, and the faith to do this work.

Blessed be God who has called you to sponsorship!

Cate-*what?*

Interestingly, the church in the twenty-first century finds itself looking to the church of the first century for guidance in helping people come to Christian faith. Currently, more and more people are raised *outside* of the faith rather than *in* the faith. For generations, the church has been baptizing the children of church members, teaching them in Sunday school, confirming them, and transferring them from church to church when they moved from one location to another. Now, however, the church is struggling to know how to introduce and nurture faith formation and spiritual development for those who have little or no previous exposure to Christian faith and life.

The early church, of course, could not rely on a base of established Christians. So early church leaders developed an extensive process of teaching or *catechizing* people who wanted to be followers of Christ. The process took years to complete and was accompanied by hearing the word, studying scripture, developing prayer, and a discernable change of life that signified a conversion to Christ. This process, known as the *catechumenate*, has found new life in the postmodern world of the twenty-first century.

The word *catechumenate* (cat-uh-CUE-men-ut) comes from a Greek word meaning "to teach orally." In the early church, this word alluded to the ways in which the faith was handed on from one to another: by hearing the word of God in scripture, in exposition, and in telling salvation stories. This was a very personal process of handing on the faith from one person to another, always within the context of the Christian community. *Inquirers* into faith eventually became *catechumens*. Catechumens learned the stories of God's saving acts in history, studied scripture, heard the word, and were joined into a type of apprenticeship with established Christians who taught them how to live the faith. After a time of such learning, if the catechumens still desired to become part of the Christian community, they became *candidates* for baptism. Then followed another period of study and personal preparation for baptism into the death and resurrection of Christ, admission to the table of the eucharist, and entering full life within the Christian community.

Heather had been "religion shopping" for some time. Raised in a Christian fundamentalist home, she spent her young adult years searching for meaning in the world religions. After exploring Asian religions and Unitarianism, she decided to try the Christian church again. There she found what had been missing: a sense of God's unconditional love. A young wife, mother, and student, she was paired with a mature single woman who helped guide her in her preparation for baptism. When she had doubts about feeling ready for baptism, her sponsor was there to talk to her about God's grace and loving acceptance of her as she was, not as she thought she should be. At the Easter Vigil Heather was baptized along with her young daughter. Two years later her husband affirmed his baptism and their infant son was baptized.

The Holy Spirit is at work calling people to conversion and to life in Christ. Conversion takes many different forms—some dramatic, some so gradual as to be hardly recognized. A modern catechumenate model has been adopted to shape the journey of people in the process of conversion and call to discipleship. The model consists of four periods:
- Inquiry
- Catechumenate
- Baptismal preparation
- Baptismal living

Movement from one period to the next is made when the inquirer discerns or recognizes a desire to move further into the catechumenate journey. Each transition is marked by a liturgical rite set within the public worship of the church. The catechumenate is by no means a private endeavor. The entire congregation is involved: as catechumenate team members, catechists or small group leaders, sponsors, or as the full assembly prays for those who are engaged in this faith journey. The catechumenate rites enable the process of conversion to engage the entire congregation in the mission of the church as people are called to baptism and beyond, following Christ's challenge in Matthew 28. The periods and rites are briefly outlined in the following chapter in order to help you understand the nature of the catechumenate and your role in it as sponsor.

A thumbnail sketch of the catechumenate process

Period of inquiry

As the Holy Spirit calls people to conversion they become *inquirers* of faith. Inquirers are searching for a place where they can ask their questions about the meaning of life, or about the nature of God, or Jesus, or what prayer is really all about. It may begin with the invitation of a friend or neighbor to attend church together, or perhaps when one begins to read a hotel Bible during a time of loneliness. It may be disguised as "church shopping." Years may pass before an inquirer steps across the threshold of a church. It may take years after the threshold has been crossed before the inquirer begins to ask the questions of a searching soul. Inquirers need people of faith to hear their questions with open hearts and without judgment, and be quick to share the joy and fulfillment of life in Christ. These inquirers need sponsors: people who have a faith story they are willing to share. Sponsors are not encyclopedias of the Christian faith, nor are they expected to be perfect models of faith. Rather, they are real people with real faith that includes peaks and valleys, who understand that faith is a lifelong journey of exploration and discovery.

The time of inquiry ends when an inquirer desires to engage in a deeper exploration of faith known as the period of the catechumenate. The transition between these two periods is marked by the rite *Welcome of Inquirers to the Catechumenate*.

During the rite of welcome, a sponsor introduces each inquirer to the congregation and the congregation acknowledges and welcomes them to join the congregation for further study of God's word and the life of faith. As the inquirer is marked with the sign of the cross, both the inquirer and the congregation are reminded that they bear the mark of Christ in all they say and do. From this time on, the inquirer may be called a *catechumen* or one who is being instructed in faith.

Period of the catechumenate

Like the period of inquiry, the period of the catechumenate is open-ended. Catechumens and sponsors commonly meet on a regular basis with a catechist or small group leader. During these meetings, the lessons from the Sunday lectionary form the basis of study and reflection. Sponsors are actively engaged in modeling the Christian faith and affirming the emerging faith in the catechumens. The disciplines of faith—study of God's word, regular worship, prayer, and ministry in daily life—are practiced and discussed throughout this period. The period of baptismal preparation begins after a catechumen expresses a desire to prepare for the sacrament of Holy Baptism. The transition between these two periods is marked by the rite *Enrollment of Candidates for Baptism.*

During the rite of enrollment the sponsor affirms the catechumen's desire to be baptized, and the congregation witnesses this intention as each candidate for baptism inscribes his or her name in a book. This book, present in the community throughout the time of the catechumens' preparation, serves as a reminder to the congregation of the preparation that is taking place in the lives of these people. The presence of the book also serves to affirm for each candidate the names of others who have also chosen to become God's children through baptism. The rite of enrollment commonly takes place on the first Sunday of Lent because Lent has historically served as the time for the candidates to prepare for Holy Baptism at the Easter Vigil or Easter Sunday. The rite may also take place at other times during the church year, such as the first Sunday of Advent when Holy Baptism will take place in January on the Baptism of Our Lord.

Period of baptismal preparation

Just as the name implies, this period of time is spent especially in preparation to receive the sacrament of Holy Baptism. During this preparation, sincere personal reflection takes place as one prepares to participate in the death and resurrection of Christ through the baptismal waters and be named as a child of God. The role of the sponsor here is to encourage and support the candidate through this time of preparation. Candidates and sponsors are prayed for by the entire congregation on a regular basis during the weeks of baptismal preparation. There may be specific rites of blessing during liturgies, in which the sponsor stands with the candidate. The end of this period is marked by the joyful celebration of Holy Baptism during the Easter Vigil or at another baptismal festival. In the baptismal rite the sponsor, as one who has accompanied the candidate through the catechumenate, will present him or her for baptism and witness the joyful sacrament. If the person is affirming his or her baptism, it still is appropriate for the sponsor to stand with the candidate.

Period of baptismal living

The ancient church called the time following baptism *mystagogy*, which means "being led into the mysteries." Today, we call this *baptismal living*. During this time catechumens explore the meaning of sacramental living and how baptism continues to be worked out in daily life. What does it mean to live as a baptized child of God? What does it mean to live a sacramental life? What does it mean to take this new life—water washed, and fed with the bread and wine, the body and blood of Christ—into my daily life? How has my life changed? How will my life continue to be transformed through word and the sacraments?

Though of course this period never ends in this lifetime, it may be lifted up and the formal catechumenate process brought to a close with the rite *Affirmation of the Vocation of the Baptized in the World*. If the baptism occurred at the Easter Vigil, this would normally be celebrated on the Day of Pentecost. The newly baptized are affirmed in their new identity as Christians and for their witness and presence in a hurting world. It is the final rite in the catechumenate process, but it is not the end of the journey. All of the work done in searching, study, reflection, prayer, worship, and action up to this point is really the pregnancy. Baptism is the moment of birth and there is a whole life of growth yet to be lived.

A thumbnail sketch of the catechumenate process:

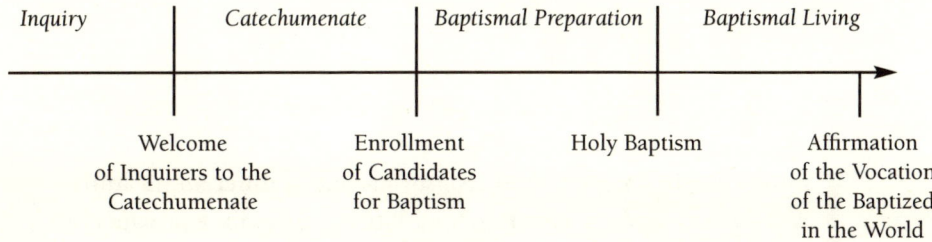

What is a sponsor?

In the present day, the word *sponsor* has many different meanings. A sponsor may be a person who invites you to join a private club and in so doing vouches for your character and accompanies you through the initiation process. A person in the recovery stage of a twelve-step program may step forward to sponsor another person beginning the long and difficult process of developing a new life. *Sponsor* often holds the same meaning as *godparent* for a child brought for baptism. A catechumenate sponsor is all of this.

You have been asked to sponsor a person who is preparing to receive the sacrament of Holy Baptism or to reaffirm their baptismal vows (this is also known as *affirmation of baptism*). You have been asked to be a sponsor because others in your congregation have recognized in you characteristics that will enable you to walk alongside another person as he or she engages in this important time of preparation. First and foremost, you are a baptized Christian who demonstrates the basic disciplines of faith. These disciplines include participation in worship on a regular basis, an interest in the study of scripture, an active prayer life, and ministry to others in daily life.

Second, you are not perfect! That may seem obvious to you, but what it means is that in the eyes of God, you are in the same boat with all Christians—a sinful being who stands condemned under

God's law, unable to earn your way into God's favor. But (again with all believers) by God's grace, you are forgiven and made right with God by the death and resurrection of Jesus Christ.

Third, you relish your life as one of God's beloved children. You have the gifts and the grace to help the inquirer, candidate, or affirmer discover the fullness of life in Christ.

The Holy Spirit is calling people to conversion to Christ and you are needed. Do not be afraid of this calling but embrace it. Conversion comes to some in a flash of light and an instant of revelation. For most, though, it comes as a process of discovery that is more a movement through time than a moment in time. You are needed to hear another person's story and to share your story. You are needed to help someone else explore the call to discipleship and help him or her develop the disciplines of faith that will serve him or her throughout life. You will be challenged by the inquirer's questions of faith, but you are not expected to be an encyclopedia of right answers. You are a person with a faith story, that is, a life story that intersects with the cross of Christ. You are asked to share your own faith story with another as together you encounter the word of God.

What does a sponsor do?

As a sponsor in the catechumenate your role is to *accompany*, *support*, and *nurture* a person who is inquiring into the Christian faith and life. In the course of inquiry, a person may eventually desire to receive the sacrament of Holy Baptism, or if a person has been baptized but has been distant from the church, he or she may desire to affirm prior baptismal promises. You will stay with that person throughout his or her time of inquiry, further study, discernment for baptism or affirmation of baptism, and beyond.

The sponsor's role is best described as a companion to the candidate. A companion walks alongside, neither ahead nor behind, and guides the candidate along the path of faith formation and spiritual development. Companionship involves both give and take. During the faith sharing and storytelling at the heart of the catechumenate, candidates offer questions and insights that engage and revitalize faith experience for the sponsor. So the journey takes both of you along the way to faith and fullness of life in Christ.

Accompany

A sponsor is a host, welcoming the inquirer to congregational life and helping the inquirer to become acquainted with the church community. Try walking into the church and intentionally taking notice

Sponsors Guide   15

of all the things that are familiar and assume that they are not familiar to the inquirer. The following ideas are ways to introduce your inquirer to church life and community:

- Sit together at worship and help the inquirer become familiar with the liturgy and the unique worship practices in your congregation.
- Introduce the inquirer to worship aids, such as assisted hearing devices and large print bulletins and hymnals, and accessible features, such as an elevator or ramps.
- Take the inquirer on a tour of the church facility. Show the meeting rooms, classrooms, rest rooms, and nursery.
- Show the inquirer which door to use to enter the church during weekdays or for evening meetings.
- Extend a personal invitation to a coffee hour after worship and to other church events.
- Introduce the inquirer to other members of the congregation.
- Identify an activity of Christian service that you can do together, such as helping in a soup kitchen or food bank or visiting homebound members of the congregation together.
- Invite the inquirer to brunch after worship or to dinner in your home.

In short, graciously help the inquirer feel comfortable in a place that may feel unfamiliar. Help him or her come to know the people and the practices of the church community.

The traditional method of bringing new members into a congregation is attendance at a new member's class for several weeks. Classes are typically led by the pastor, and the newcomers (inquirers) become acquainted with the pastor and other newcomers. After completing the class, those who are transferring membership and those affirming their baptism stand in front of the congregation and are received into membership. Because they may have only become acquainted with others in their class, the new members might look out into the congregation and see only strangers. You can help them feel welcome into the community long before they are baptized or affirm their baptism. In the catechumenate, you are the bridge that links the congregation and the inquirer.

Link the candidates to the worshiping community. The rites of the catechumenate mark the movement of the inquirer along the faith journey. The action of the rites will call upon you to do several things. At the entrance to the nave, you will present the inquirer by name to the congregation for the rite of welcome. Later in the service you will trace the cross on the inquirer's body: forehead, ears, eyes, lips, heart, shoulders, hand, and feet as he or she is given the sign of the gospel. You will lay your hands on the inquirer's head as prayers of blessing are spoken. In the rite of enrollment for baptism, you will affirm his or her desire to be baptized. At the time of baptism you will stand with the candidate, a visible sign of your support and the constant presence of the church community.

Sponsors are the physical connection—the voice, the face, the hands, the touch—that connects the inquirers to the whole body of Christ. With sponsors by their side, inquirers are connected to the existing congregation in a real and tangible way while still in the catechumenate process. Because of the companionship and hospitality extended by sponsors, candidates are likely to be fully integrated into the life of the congregation by the time of their baptism.

Support

The body of Christ is large and complex, extending far beyond the physical confines of any church building. It is in this community of Christ that Christians come to faith and fullness of life. Support for one another is always important, but it is especially so for those who are being called to conversion to Christ. You and your candidate should be in regular contact with each other. Check in with him or her on a regular basis. If a catechetical session is missed, you might call the candidate or drop by with notes from the session and discuss the topic or scripture passage together. You may choose to share devotional materials or inspirational reading or tapes with your candidate. Topics for casual conversation might include current events or ethical situations that arise in everyday life. Explore the call of discipleship together and share the blessings of living as a child of God. Your openness to freely share personal experiences will set the stage for your candidate to fully explore the call to Christian living.

Practice prayer. Regular prayer with and for your candidate is an exceptional opportunity for you as a sponsor. Daily prayer helps you focus on the candidate's spiritual needs. When your candidate knows that prayers are being brought before God daily on his or her behalf, he or she will begin to experience the power of the Holy Spirit to know and trust God. It is humbling for a sponsor to witness the seeds of faith begin to grow in the candidate.

In addition to daily prayer, modeling prayer in small group catechetical sessions helps candidates learn how to pray. They may only be able to begin with a word or phrase, but as they witness and participate in prayer, they will learn ways to let their requests be made known to God and their joys be expressed in thanksgiving. Prayer enriches both the lives of those who pray and those for whom the prayers are offered.

Respect confidentiality. As your relationship grows, it is your responsibility to set confidentiality parameters. Small group discussion rules prohibit any conversation that takes place within the group from going outside the group. The same is true with the sponsor/candidate relationship. As trust develops and lives are shared, your candidate should feel confident that conversations with you will not be a topic of discussion during your coffee break at work, or at the next weekly Bible study.

You can be a confidant, but not a therapist. If issues of personal safety or emotional or psychological well-being surface, speak frankly to the candidate about your concern for the candidate's well-being. Encourage him or her to speak with the pastor or a professional counselor. If the candidate is reluctant to do so, you may offer to make this contact with the candidate's permission.

Nurture

Sponsors nurture candidates by actively listening to questions, observations, insights, and emerging expressions of faith as they are revealed in catechetical groups or casual conversation. As a companion along the journey of faith formation, you will find that freely sharing the valleys and peaks of your own life experiences will be as useful in nurturing faith as consulting theological resources to find the right answer. It is likely that the candidate will raise questions for which you have no answer. Be frank and honest with the candidate when this happens. Some questions call for a response from faith and experience; others require factual or informational answers. You are the sounding board for the exploration of faith questions. Answers to questions are important, and catechists and clergy have a responsibility to see that questions of scripture or doctrine are openly received and addressed. Nurturing a developing faith, however, involves leading a person along a path in a way that enables the discovery of the way to Jesus.

Give your most precious gift: your time and yourself. Time is always in short supply and it may seem impossible to give any more time to another church activity. Sponsorship does require time and commitment. Remember, though, that as one gives, one also receives. Time and time again, those who have been catechumenate sponsors report that the regular rhythm of catechetical meetings becomes a part of the rhythm of life. The disciplines of study, worship, and prayer, along with the relationship that develops with the candidate are well worth the investment of time and self. Sponsors frequently report that this intentional time of faith formation spent with a candidate has been as important for the sponsors themselves as for the candidate. You may find that sponsorship provides an opportunity to take a sabbatical from other commitments in order to focus on your own faith formation and spiritual development.

How are sponsor matches made?

The goal of those who identify and recruit sponsors is to make a match that will enhance the faith journey of the inquirer. The leadership team in your congregation gives careful consideration to the selection of sponsors for the inquirers. You might be asked to sponsor someone who shares similar interests and is at a similar station in life. Mike and Eileen began attending church with their three young children because Eileen wanted to give her children the moral and spiritual upbringing she had received. Mike had never been baptized and had no church upbringing. They were paired with Brent and Lucy and their young children. As it turned out, their children attended the same preschool. Mike "apprenticed the faith" with Brent, who sponsored him in his preparation for baptism. Lucy and Eileen found common ground between them. These couples began a lasting relationship as friends and mutual support, grounded in the faith of the church.

A young, single inquirer may wish to be sponsored by someone much like himself, as with Martin and Jeff. Both single, far from home and family and in the stressful world of high-tech development, they formed a bond that provided support within the faith community, but also in their professional and social lives. Others might prefer to be sponsored in a different way. Ruth lived her life in many Lutheran churches interspersed with periods of no church membership. She intended to join the congregation by affirmation of baptism and was paired with a sponsor in a similar life station: about 40 years old, divorced, and childless. The sponsors' assignment worked okay, but Ruth later said that she would have preferred to be sponsored by a family with children because she missed that element of her own life.

Choosing the best match really rests on the needs of the inquirer. The gifts you bring to sponsorship and the known needs of the inquirer were considered prayerfully before you were asked to be a sponsor. Spiritual development is the main goal of the pairing. Don't feel guilty if you don't become best buddies. Great sponsors are sometimes just casual friends with their candidates. Try not to push a relationship beyond its natural development. Be natural and authentic.

Congregational support for sponsors

Sponsoring is a demanding role, both personally and spiritually. As you accompany, support, and nurture your candidate, the congregation will support you in several ways.

You should fully understand the catechumenate process and your role in it as sponsor. An introductory meeting is a helpful way to explain the catechumenate process, discuss adult baptism and affirmation of baptism, and describe the very important role of the sponsor in the process. Ask questions of your leadership team. Resource materials such as a sponsor description, catechumenate meeting schedule, and biographical candidate information, including address and phone number, should be available. Ask whom you should contact if further questions arise.

Your leadership team may schedule regular meeting times for sponsors to check in with the team. Here are some possible topics for discussion.

- How is the process going for you?
- How do you perceive the process is going for your candidate?
- Are there particular concerns or unanswered questions that need to be addressed?
- How is the sponsor's role fitting?
- How are the catechetical groups doing?

- What has been the greatest challenge so far?
- What has been the biggest blessing?
- Are there other ways in which the leadership team can help you in your role?

A simple prayer service for sponsors may be offered occasionally. The liturgy of evening prayer could be used, but a full liturgy is not necessary. After the scripture readings, individual prayers may be offered that include petitions for the sponsor's continuing faith journey, personal needs and requests, as well as guidance for his or her role as a sponsor in the catechumenate.

It is important that the supportive power of prayer be upheld before all people involved in the catechumenate, including the entire congregation. Just as the candidates are regularly prayed for by the worshiping community during the prayers of the church, the sponsors should be named in prayer also. The work of sponsorship can be exhilarating and exhausting, uplifting and challenging. The support of the entire congregation is necessary for all who are on the catechumenate journey.

Sponsorship and renewal

Helen, baptized into the congregation as an infant and now a senior member in the same congregation, has sponsored several candidates, mostly young women. Helen has said many times that she enjoys being a sponsor because it gives her the opportunity to get to know newcomers. She especially likes sponsoring young mothers because of the richness that mixed generations can share. She finds special moments of evangelism when she can share her faith story and in so doing make God's story more personal. Helen's summary of the sponsor's role is that it has been the most important thing she has ever done in her long life of faith and service in the church.

For sponsors, the opportunity to be engaged in the faith development of individuals seeking to know Christ makes acutely clear the mission of the church. Church membership is about more than meeting the mortgage or recruiting for various positions of leadership. It is essentially about the witness of Christ in the world. The Great Commission in Matthew 28 calls all Christians to "make disciples of all nations." This is the mission of the church. You may discover that while you are performing the role of sponsor your own faith is renewed.

By the time Pentecost and the rite *Affirmation of the Vocation of the*

Baptized in the World have taken place, the entire assembly has prayed for, supported, and nurtured sponsors and candidates throughout the many months of the catechumenate. The people of the catechumenate have been named in catechumenal liturgical rites, the weekly prayers of the church, and newsletter articles and bulletin announcements. There is no mistaking that something special has been happening. The adults who diligently prepared to receive the sacrament of Holy Baptism or to publicly affirm their baptism have moved the entire congregation by their profession of faith. As witnesses to this faith, the congregation's members have renewed their own confession and commitment to faith. As the catechumenate process individually transforms a congregation's members, so the mission of the church is transformed.

Affirmation of baptism

Candidates for affirmation of baptism who have been away from the church each come with a unique history with the church. These are the children that God has received by Holy Baptism. Like the prodigal son, their birthright in the family of God has never been lost. Their return to the family has been prayed for, hoped for, and anxiously awaited. With open arms, we greet them, "Welcome home!"

Their stories are all different. Some were brought for baptism as infants, but not taught the way of the church and Christian living. For them, church may be a new or unfamiliar place and they may be wary of church people. Others have fallen away from the church due to disinterest, disagreements, or disappointment. Some may be reconnecting to the church because of marriage or the birth of a child, or because of a major life trauma, such as divorce, personal tragedy, or loss of a loved one. These baptized persons need to be gently brought back home to the church where life as God's children and members of the Christian community began.

The journey of some affirmers will closely mirror those who have never been baptized. For others, there may be issues of pain and hurt from previous church experiences that need to be uncovered and healed before the affirmer can be fully reconciled with the church and able to honestly affirm their baptismal promises. The catechumenate allows for this reflection and healing. As a sponsor, whether for affirmers or for the unbaptized, your role is to accompany, nurture, and support those who are coming to the faith and fullness of life offered through the community of the church.

A final word

The catechumenate is a gift to the church that gathers the faith community around the invitation to know Christ. Life with Christ begins and ends at the baptismal font. In between, we walk, run, stand still, and sometimes lose our way along the journey of faith. There are others who travel with us. They accompany, encourage, challenge, listen, and pray. They show us the way when we are lost, and they never let go. They personally claim their call to discipleship and prayerfully accompany others, both those coming to the font of grace and those who are coming home to the refreshing and life-giving waters of baptism and to the community that claims them in Christ. They are the community of saints. In the catechumenate we call them sponsors.

Top ten ideas for sponsors

- Pray for your candidate every day.
- Invite your candidate to a coffee hour or an adult education class.
- Does your candidate have children? Offer to sit with them one Sunday.
- Invite your candidate to attend a parish activity with you.
- Give your candidate a call on a random day just to say you are thinking of him or her.
- Check in by phone with your candidate when a catechumenate meeting is missed.
- Tell your candidate about when you joined the congregation.
- Volunteer at a local food bank or homeless shelter with your candidate.
- Introduce your candidate to at least three members of the congregation each week.
- Pray for your candidate every day.

Appendix A

Sponsors Assist Those Being Baptized

Principle

20   Both adults and infants benefit from having baptismal sponsors. The primary role of the sponsors is to guide and accompany the candidates and, so far as possible, their families in the process of instruction and Baptism. They help the baptized join in the life and work of the community of believers for the sake of the world.

Application 20A   Congregations are encouraged to select at least one sponsor from among the congregational members for each candidate for Baptism. . . . Choosing and preparing sponsors requires thoughtful consideration and includes participation by pastors or other congregational leaders. . . .

Background 20C   . . . In the case of the baptism of an adult, this sponsor accompanies the candidate throughout the catechumenate, in prayer and in mutual learning, assisting the newly baptized adult to join in the ministry and mission of this community.

Application 20D   The entire congregation prays for those preparing for Baptism, welcomes the newly baptized, and provides assistance to sponsors.

Excerpt from The Use of the Means of Grace: A Statement on the Practice of Word and Sacrament. *Adopted for guidance and practice by the Evangelical Lutheran Church in America.*

Resources for Prayer

At the beginning of the study of the word

O God,
open my eyes that I might see you;
open my ears that I might hear you;
open my heart that I might know you. Amen

At the conclusion of the study of the word

Living God, may your word live in my heart and in my thoughts, in what I say and what I do. Amen

A prayer for those who do not know Christ

Almighty God, you know the heart of every person. Send your Holy Spirit to those who long to hear your word of forgiveness and freedom, hope, and peace. Awaken in them a desire to know you and prepare your people to receive them with love and grace. In the name of Christ our Lord. Amen

A prayer for inquirers

Gracious God, through your Holy Spirit you reach out to all people. We thank you for the presence among us of those who are searching for answers for their lives. Bless them with your love, and give us openness to share with each other our questions and our faith. We pray in the name of your Son, Jesus Christ our Lord. Amen

A prayer for catechumens

You, O God, are the potter, and we are the clay. You have created us and continue gently to shape us. Guide the catechumens among us, as well as their sponsors and catechists. Give them wisdom and patience, and lead them toward greater love for you, who have shown your love through your Son, Jesus Christ our Lord. Amen

Appendix B

A prayer for candidates

Almighty and eternal God, you continually bless the church with new members. Increase the faith and understanding of those preparing for baptism. Give them a new birth as your children, and keep them in the faith and communion of your holy church. We ask this through Christ our Lord. Amen

A prayer for the newly baptized

God, the Father of our Lord Jesus Christ, we give you thanks for freeing your sons and daughters from the power of sin and for raising them up to a new life through this holy sacrament. Pour your Holy Spirit upon <u>name</u>: the spirit of wisdom and understanding, the spirit of counsel and might, the spirit of knowledge and the fear of the Lord, the spirit of joy in your presence. Amen

A prayer for those who have affirmed their baptism

Gracious Lord, through water and the Spirit you have made these men and women your own. You forgave them all their sins and brought them to newness of life. Continue to strengthen them with the Holy Spirit, and daily increase in them your gifts of grace: the spirit of wisdom and understanding, the spirit of counsel and might, the spirit of knowledge and the fear of the Lord, the spirit of joy in your presence; through Jesus Christ, your Son, our Lord. Amen